ISAAC ASIMOV'S
LIBRARY OF THE UNIVERSE

COMETS AND METEORS

by Isaac Asimov

DELL YEARLING   NONFICTION

Published by
Dell Publishing
a division of
Bantam Doubleday Dell Publishing Group, Inc.
666 Fifth Avenue
New York, New York   10103

This edition was first published in the United States and Canada in 1990
by Gareth Stevens, Inc.

Technical advisers and consulting editors: Fran Millhouser, Julian Baum, and Francis Reddy

ISBN: 0-440-40450-9

Reprinted by arrangement with Gareth Stevens, Inc.

Printed in the United States of America
November 1991

10 9 8 7 6 5 4 3 2 1

CONTENTS

Nowadays, we have seen planets up close, all the way to distant Uranus and Neptune. We have mapped Venus through its clouds. We have seen the rings around Neptune and the ice volcanoes on Triton, one of Neptune's moons. We have detected strange objects no one knew anything about till recently: quasars, pulsars, black holes. We have studied stars not only by the light they give out, but by other kinds of radiation: infrared, ultraviolet, x-rays, radio waves. We have even detected tiny particles called neutrinos that are given off by the stars.

Some astronomical objects have been known from very ancient times, however. People have always seen comets in the sky and wondered about them. They were often terrified by them. They also saw "shooting stars," or meteors, and wondered if they were stars that had come loose and fallen. In this book, let's take a look at comets and meteors.

Isaac Asimov

What Is a Comet?

To most of us, a comet looks like a hazy patch in the sky. This object, made of ice, rock, and gas, appears as a very dim haze at the start, and it slowly moves among the stars from night to night, getting brighter, then fading again till it disappears.

The hazy patch stretches out into a "tail" that always points away from the direction of the Sun. The tail gets longer as the comet grows brighter, until it sometimes stretches far across the sky. Then the tail shortens and fades.

A tail is but one of many things people think of when they see a comet. People have imagined a comet as a woman's head with long hair streaming behind. And in fact, the word "comet" comes from a Greek word meaning "hair."

Opposite: Comet Ikeya-Seki was photographed in the early morning sky near Tucson, Arizona, in 1965.

Right: a woman's head with long hair streaming behind — a favorite image of a comet. Comets have long meant many things to many people.

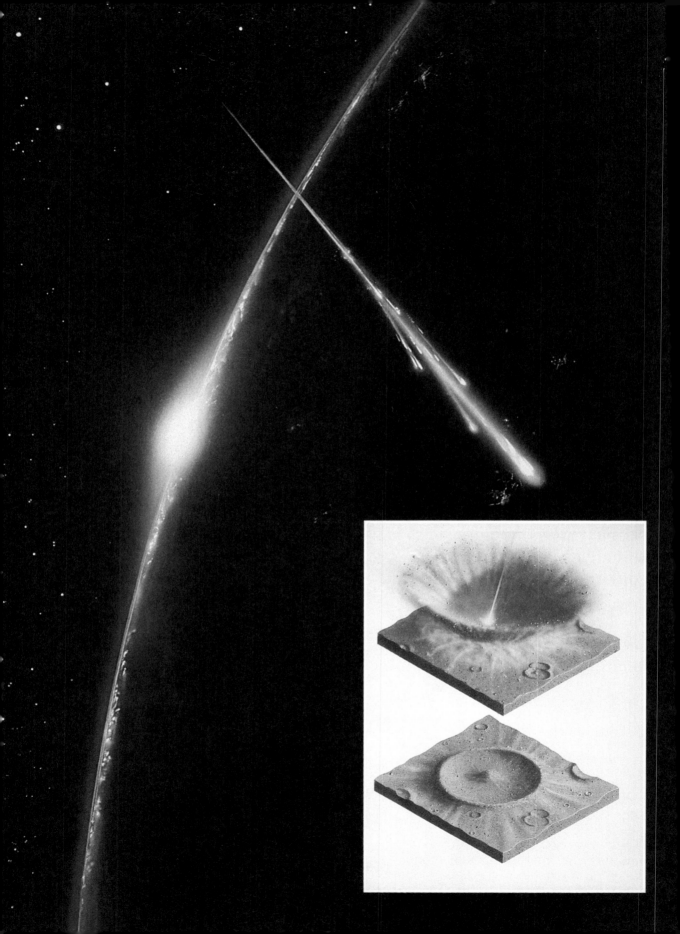

What Is a Meteor?

Meteors don't last very long in the sky, but like comets, they have fascinated people — and even frightened them — for centuries.

Meteors look like stars that move across the sky for some distance and then disappear. Any clear Moonless night, especially after midnight, you can see such "shooting stars." Sometimes you can see dozens in a single night. Usually, meteors are quite dim, but sometimes they are bright and are called "fireballs."

Meteors are not really stars, though, and the real stars always stay in the sky — no matter how many "shooting stars" streak across the sky! The word "meteor" comes from the Greek words meaning "things in the air," and this is exactly what meteors are — shining objects streaking through Earth's atmosphere.

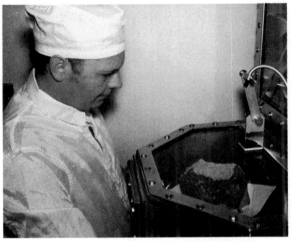

An Antarctic find: Scientists study a possible meteorite from Mars.

Opposite: In this artist's concept, a fireball briefly brightens the early morning sky. Skywatchers on Earth below have witnessed a brilliant "shooting star."

Inset, opposite: If the rock that creates a meteor travels all the way to the ground without burning up, it strikes the Earth and becomes a meteorite. Very large meteorites have dug out craters on Earth, the Moon, Mars, and other worlds.

**Meteorites —
"moonoids" in disguise?**

Some meteorites contain the same materials — and the same proportion of materials — that make up Moon rocks. When meteoroids bombarded the Moon and gouged out craters there, the Moon's weak gravity allowed some of the material to be knocked off the Moon entirely. It may be that some of the meteorites found on Earth are really Moon rocks. A very few meteorites include gases with the make-up of the Martian atmosphere, so there may be Mars rocks on Earth, too.

7

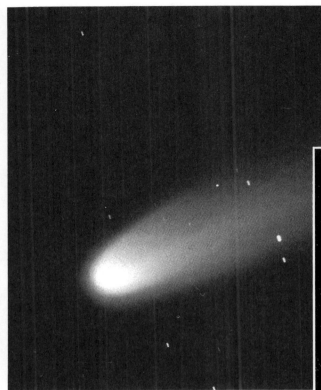

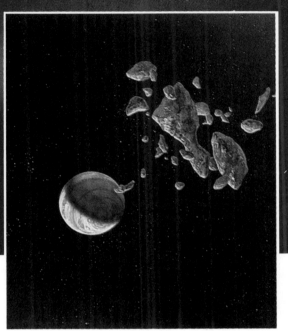

Above: Comet Bennett, a bright comet that appeared in 1969, as seen through a telescope.

Opposite: A meteor shower occurs when our planet passes through the dusty path of a comet.

The remains of a burned-out comet. Tiny dust particles trail along its orbit, creating meteors when Earth runs into them.

Comets and Meteor Showers

In some ways, comets and certain kinds of meteors are related. Here's how this works. The haze of a comet contains countless particles of dust. Following the path of the comet, this dust scatters through space. Some of this dust is concentrated into large clumps.

Every once in a while, Earth may pass through such clumps. The dust particles then speed rapidly through Earth's atmosphere. As a result of friction with the atmosphere, the particles heat up, become white hot, and glow. The result is a "meteor shower." There are certain times of certain years when people watch the sky to see such showers. They see many meteors streaking across the sky.

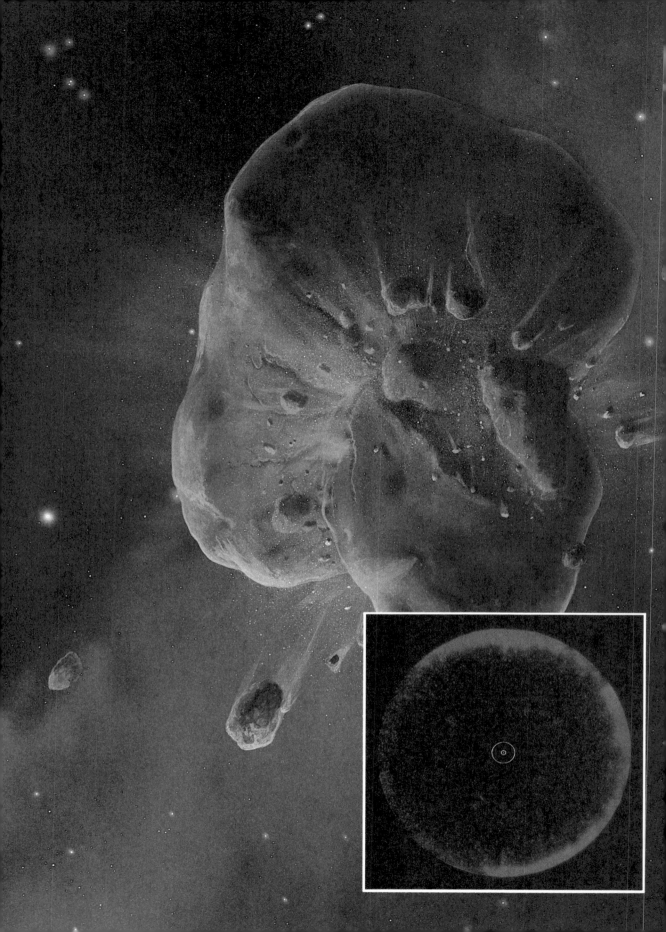

Comets — Where Do They Come From?

Many comets have been seen throughout human history, and they have always seemed to appear out of nowhere. In 1950, an astronomer, Jan Oort, figured out that there must be trillions of comets circling the Sun at a huge distance. This comet cloud, called the Oort Cloud, consists of icy bodies containing rocky dust.

Some of the bodies may have a rocky center. Sometimes, two comets may collide, or a comet may be pulled at by a distant star. A comet's motion may then slow and it will "fall" toward the Sun. As it approaches the Sun, the ice warms and forms a dusty vapor, which is what we see from Earth.

Opposite: a rare event in deep space: Two comets collide in the Oort Cloud. They may slow down enough to begin the long fall to the Sun, appearing in our skies millions of years from now.

Inset, opposite: a diagram of the Oort Cloud, the shell of trillions of comets that surrounds the Solar system. (Pluto's orbit is the large yellow circle.)

Right: Dutch astronomer Jan Oort (left), who suggested the existence of a cloud of comets after studying the motions of dozens of comets.

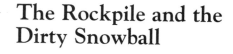

The Rockpile and the Dirty Snowball

Since comets are made up of icy materials and rocky dust, they are sometimes called "dirty snowballs." But not all meteors are caused by comet dust. Many meteors are caused by tiny asteroids or asteroid-like objects made of rock and metal speeding through space. While they are in space, they are called meteoroids.

Once meteoroids strike the atmosphere and become white hot, they are called meteors. Most meteors are tiny and heat entirely into vapor. But some are large enough so they don't completely burn up. Bits of them survive and strike Earth's surface. These pieces are called meteorites.

A slice through a meteorite. Only the outer crust is affected by its fiery fall to Earth. The rest of the rock provides scientists with clues about the early days of the Solar system.

A dirty snowball, our best model of a comet. Bits of rock and dust are mixed into a ball of ice. When the ice ball warms near the Sun, part of it turns to gas and carries the dust into space.

Right: another meteorite find in Antarctica! Some 7,000 samples have been discovered here since the 1960s.

**Finding meteorites —
one trick of the trade**

Unless you see a meteorite actually fall, you're not likely to find one just by looking around. Most are too much like ordinary rocks — and you can't go around checking every rock near you for signs of its being a meteorite! The one exception — Arctic and Antarctic regions, with their large, remote, ice-covered surfaces. A piece of rock on top of the ice would just about have to be a meteorite. There's really no other way it could have gotten there!

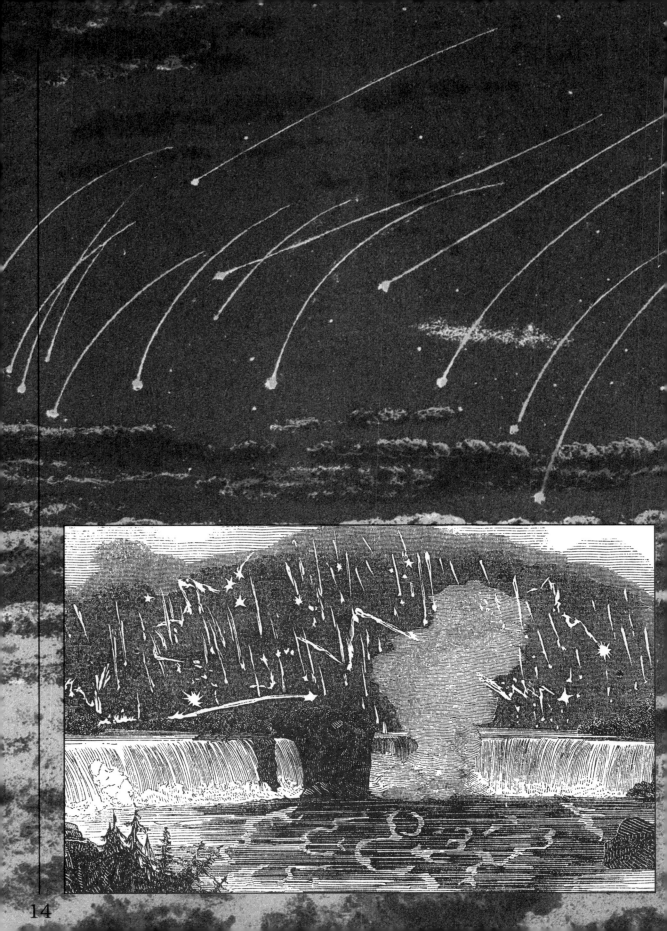

The Big Meteor Shower

Today we accept the idea of stones falling from the sky. But reports of meteor sightings weren't always taken seriously. In 1833, however, Earth passed through a huge collection of tiny dust particles in space. As many as 200,000 meteors were seen during one night!

It was the biggest meteor shower ever reported. Some people thought it was the end of the world and that all the stars had fallen from the sky. The next night, however, all the stars were still there. Reports of the shower got everyone thinking about meteors, and pretty soon it was clear that stones <u>could</u> fall from the sky.

Background: a unique location for observing a meteor shower — a balloon!

Inset, opposite: the great meteor shower of 1833, as seen from Niagara Falls.

15

The Great Comets

Like meteoroids, comets come in a variety of sizes and shapes. Some comets are quite large. In 1811, a huge comet appeared in the sky. Its head was a cloud of dust that was larger than the Sun, and it had a tail that stretched for millions of miles. The tail consisted entirely of scattered dust, and it amounted to nothing — but it looked impressive.

Other large comets appeared in 1861, in 1882, and in 1910. Comets that appeared in 1861 and in 1910 had tails that appeared to stretch halfway across the sky.

Since 1910, there have been a few bright comets, but none like the real giants of the century before 1910. The truth is that hardly anyone living today has ever seen a really spectacular comet.

Opposite: Donati's Comet hangs over Paris, France.

Inset, opposite: the splendid tail of Comet Seki-Lines of 1962.

Below: The most famous comet of all, Halley, as it appeared in 1910.

Comet flops and flying colors

Sometimes astronomers are fooled into thinking a far-off comet will be a big one. Because Comet Kohoutek was seen far off in 1973, everyone expected it would be a huge, bright comet. It turned out to be a complete flop. On the other hand, Comet West, from which little was expected, turned out to be quite bright. Perhaps a lot depends on how rocky a comet is. A thick, rocky crust might cause the comet to brighten far less than expected as it nears the Sun.

Halley's Comet

After Isaac Newton worked out the Law of Gravity in 1687, his friend Edmund Halley became fascinated with comets. In 1682, a comet had crossed the sky, following the same path as comets in 1531 and 1607.

Using the Law of Gravity, Halley showed that what looked like three comets was actually the same comet traveling around the Sun in a long orbit and returning about every 76 years. He predicted the comet would return in 1758 and take its usual path across the sky. Halley's prediction was nearly right on target. In 1759, the comet returned, and it has come to be known as "Halley's Comet" for that reason. Since then, it has returned in 1835, 1910, and 1986.

Background: a 15th-century drawing of Halley's Comet.

Inset: a sketch of Halley's appearance in the 17th century.

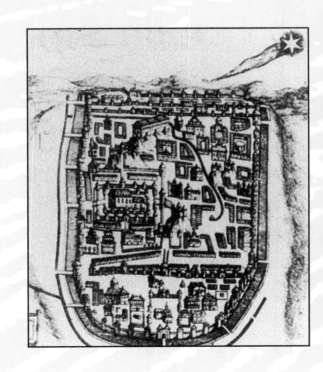

EDMUNDUS HALLEIUS R.S.S.

Edmund Halley, the 18th-century astronomer who became the first person to predict a comet's return.

The Giotto space probe gave us our first up-close view of a comet. This picture shows the core of Halley's Comet as seen from some 16,000 miles (26,000 km) away.

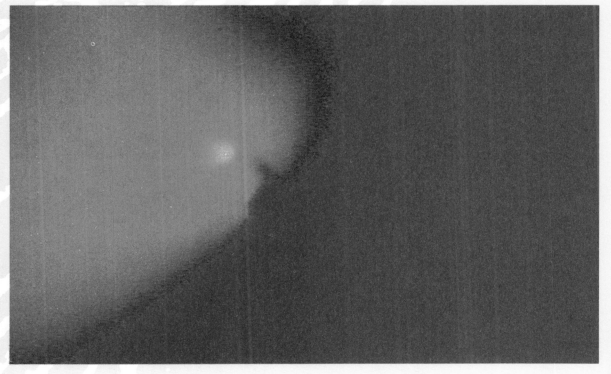

Living in Fear of the Comet

Before Halley figured out a comet's orbit, people thought that comets were a heavenly sign of coming events on Earth. And because the tail looked like the hair of a wailing woman, or like a sword, they thought it meant war and disaster.

When a big comet appeared, crowds of people would pray and church bells would ring. Even in recent times, people have panicked. In 1910, it seemed that Earth would pass through the tail of Halley's Comet. Many people were afraid the world would come to an end. But like the tail of every other comet, Halley's tail is just dust. Nothing at all happened to Earth.

A humorous look at a grim thought: A comet destroys Earth while the "Man in the Moon" smiles on.

Background: Oh, no! It's a c-c-comet! Even in modern times (Paris, 1811), many people were afraid that comets brought disaster.

Inset: Montezuma, ruler of the Aztecs, was frightened by a comet in 1520.

**Comets —
a prediction of doom?**

Halley's Comet appeared in AD 66; four years later, the Jews revolted against Rome and were crushed. It appeared in 1066 and the Saxons of England were defeated by William the Conquerer. It appeared in 1456, and the Turks mopped out the very last bits of the Roman Empire. Whenever <u>any</u> comet appears, there is some sort of war, or death of a king, or other disaster. Isn't that amazing? No, it isn't, because whenever <u>no</u> comet appears, disaster also strikes.

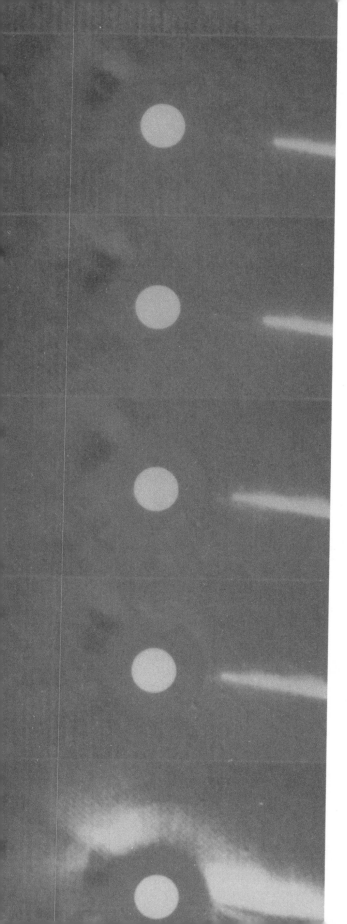

The Death of Comets

Every time a comet moves about the Sun, some of its icy material evaporates to form the cloud of dust and the tail. This material never comes back to the comet. Over the years the comet shrinks, and after returning a few hundred or a few thousand times, all its icy material is gone.

The rocky core that remains may resemble little more than one more meteoroid sailing through the cosmos. If there is no rocky core, the comet vanishes altogether and leaves nothing but a cloud of dust.

Astronomers have actually watched a comet break up. Once a comet breaks up, it no longer keeps its scheduled appointments with Earth. The comet has died.

Left: A comet collides with the Sun in this sequence of photos taken by a space-borne camera designed to monitor the Sun's activity. The pictures, taken in 1979, show Comet Howard-Koomen-Michels racing closer to the Sun. Only a cloud of dust and gas emerges from the other side.

Inset, opposite: an artist's rendition of the dusty remains of a comet plunging into the Sun's surface.

Opposite: Although this comet is no closer to the Sun than the planet Saturn, the Sun's heat is already changing it. The comet's ice is turning to gas and has begun to form a faint tail.

Sun-grazers and kamikaze comets

Some comets "fall" so close to the Sun that they skim only a million miles (1.6 million km) or less above its surface. The Sun's heat might be enough to break these "Sun-grazers" into a string of four or five fragments that might skim by the Sun on their return visit, like beads on a necklace. Astronomers have even seen comets plunge <u>into</u> the Sun. What makes comets "drop" from the distant Oort Cloud and act like this so near the Sun? We don't know for sure.

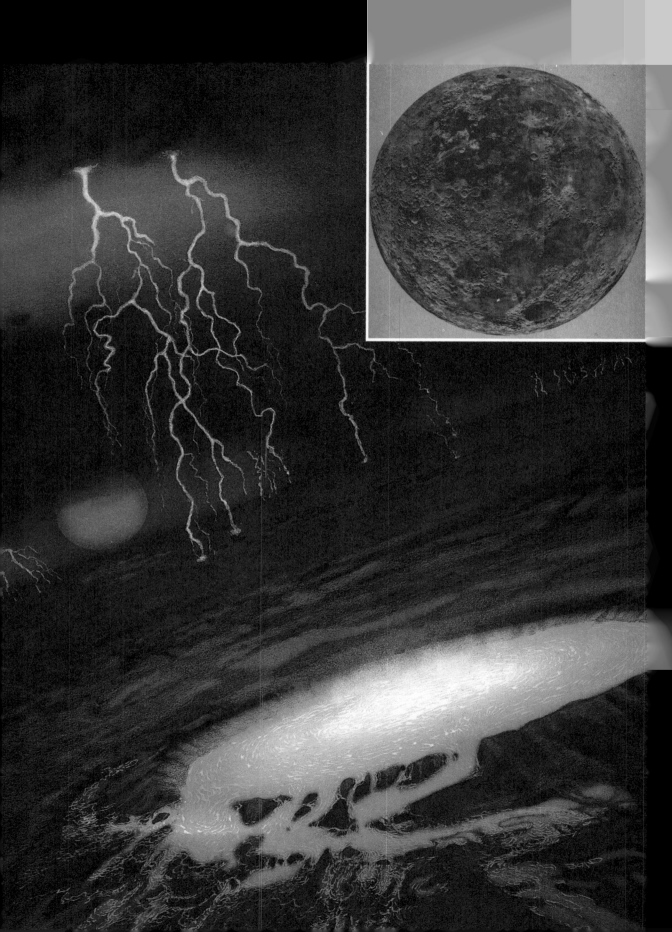

The Unthinkable

Earth has long been pelted by countless objects from space — most of them burning up harmlessly in our atmosphere as fiery meteors. Some scientists even suggest that Earth is under daily bombardment by thousands of minicomets. These minicomets, over billions of years, would have "flown in" enough water to fill Earth's oceans, and they might even account for the extinction of the dinosaurs.

While scientists argue over minicomets, we can say for sure that sometimes a <u>sizable</u> meteoroid or comet hits Earth's surface. There is a crater about three-quarters of a mile (1.2 km) wide in Arizona where a meteoroid may have struck between 15,000 and 40,000 years ago. In 1908, a small comet may have struck in the middle of Siberia and knocked down a forest of trees. If such an impact had taken place on a city, millions of people would have been killed.

On Earth, the craters formed by such impacts are slowly filled in by the action of wind, water, and life. On airless worlds, like the Moon, the surface is covered with craters that are never filled in.

Both the young Earth and Moon were pelted by comets and asteroids shortly after they formed. Opposite: The atmosphere, oceans, and volcanic activity of our planet erased most of Earth's craters. On the airless Moon, however (inset), the surface has remained mostly unchanged for billions of years. Below: Did a comet signal the beginning of the end for the dinosaurs?

Did comets kill the dinosaurs?

When scientists dig up rocks that are 65 million years old, they find unusual amounts of the rare metal iridium. Such iridium may have come from an object striking Earth. It was just 65 million years ago that dinosaurs vanished from the planet. Could a comet or meteorite impact have created the kind of disaster that killed them? Scientists aren't sure. Might another comet or meteorite strike wipe out other forms of life, including human beings, some day?

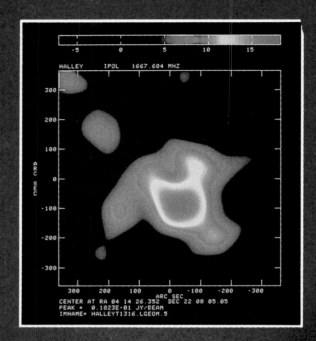

HALLEY   IPOL   1667.604 MHZ

CENTER AT RA 04 14 26.352   DEC 22 08 05.05
PEAK = 0.1823E-01 JY/BEAM
IMNAME= HALLEYT1316.LGEOM.5

The Probes — Playing on Halley's Home Court

When Halley's Comet returned in 1986, it was met by several rocket probes, including two Japanese probes, the two Soviet Vegas, and the European Space Agency (ESA) Giotto craft.

These probes sent loads of exciting information and pictures back to Earth. We now know, for example, that Halley was larger than had been thought — about the size and shape of Manhattan! And Halley was as dark as coal. Its surface ice had evaporated, but the solid dust remained mostly behind, so it was a <u>very</u> dirty snowball. At the place where ice was still evaporating — several spots where the rocky shell was weak and had cracked — jets of gas and dust shot out.

Halley's dust contained chemicals that have told us some things about interstellar space and the early days of our Solar system. With more comet encounters planned for the future, scientists expect comets to act as "probes" carrying all sorts of news about the cosmos into our Solar neighborhood.

Opposite: This composite of 60 Giotto images of Halley's Comet reveals the gas jets on its surface. Inset: a picture of Halley obtained by radio telescope.

Below: A future comet mission will place a space probe in orbit around the comet's nucleus to monitor changes as the comet circles the Sun.

Fact File: Halley's Comet Through the Ages

Throughout recorded history, humans have associated comets with changing luck (mostly for the bad) and with foretelling the future. But not everyone has been content to be mystified by these fiery apparitions in the sky. For example, the Babylonians suspected that comets were celestial bodies like planets or groups of stars. And by the 1400s and 1500s, European astronomers began treating comets calmly as an astronomical phenomenon.

In 1682, Edmund Halley had an idea that would affect people's thinking about comets to this very day. His idea? — that comets might travel in elliptical

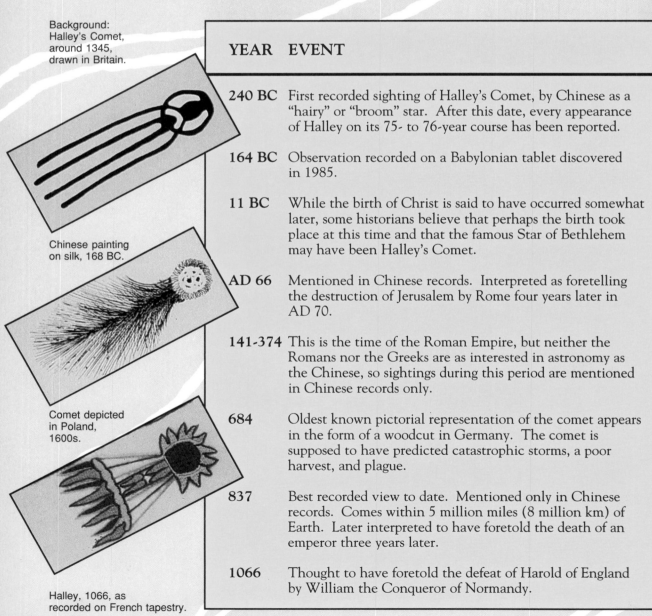

Background: Halley's Comet, around 1345, drawn in Britain.

Chinese painting on silk, 168 BC.

Comet depicted in Poland, 1600s.

Halley, 1066, as recorded on French tapestry.

YEAR	EVENT
240 BC	First recorded sighting of Halley's Comet, by Chinese as a "hairy" or "broom" star. After this date, every appearance of Halley on its 75- to 76-year course has been reported.
164 BC	Observation recorded on a Babylonian tablet discovered in 1985.
11 BC	While the birth of Christ is said to have occurred somewhat later, some historians believe that perhaps the birth took place at this time and that the famous Star of Bethlehem may have been Halley's Comet.
AD 66	Mentioned in Chinese records. Interpreted as foretelling the destruction of Jerusalem by Rome four years later in AD 70.
141-374	This is the time of the Roman Empire, but neither the Romans nor the Greeks are as interested in astronomy as the Chinese, so sightings during this period are mentioned in Chinese records only.
684	Oldest known pictorial representation of the comet appears in the form of a woodcut in Germany. The comet is supposed to have predicted catastrophic storms, a poor harvest, and plague.
837	Best recorded view to date. Mentioned only in Chinese records. Comes within 5 million miles (8 million km) of Earth. Later interpreted to have foretold the death of an emperor three years later.
1066	Thought to have foretold the defeat of Harold of England by William the Conqueror of Normandy.

28

paths similar to those of the planets. This meant that comets could be tracked and that their visits could be calculated and even predicted.

Halley used Newton's Law of Gravity to predict that a comet which had passed by Earth in 1607 and in 1682 would return in 1758. Actually, it returned in 1759. It was one year "late" because it had passed near Jupiter, whose strong gravity slowed the comet down. But 1759 was close enough. Halley's prediction was an accurate one, and the comet was named in his honor. The chart on these two pages shows other notable events in the history of sightings of perhaps the world's favorite comet, Halley.

YEAR   EVENT

1456   At the request of the pope, Europeans pray against it as an evil omen. Seen as a heavenly comment on the fall of Constantinople to the Turks three years before.

1682   Noted by Edmund Halley, who uses prior sightings and Newton's Law of Gravity to predict the next arrival for 1758.

1759   Halley's first predicted arrival. It is one year off of the original estimate because comet passes close to the large planets in our Solar system.

1835   Thanks in part to astronomers' ability to predict its arrival, for the first time the average person begins to enjoy watching Halley's Comet and people's curiosity begins to replace their fear.

1910   Comet is examined scientifically. Even so, people buy "comet pills" to protect them against the "evil" effects of the comet. Though the pills do nothing, neither does the comet. At this sighting, the tail stretches across the sky.

1986   In some ways the most disappointing sighting in 2,000 years. The comet spends its brightest time farthest away from Earth, so our view of Halley is faint when it reaches its closest distance from Earth on April 10. But thanks to modern methods of gathering information, including the rocket probes sent to meet Halley from Earth, astronomers gather lots of exciting information about Halley and comets in general. This is also an important sighting in other ways, as it has become a sign of international scientific cooperation.

Italian painting, by Giotto, 1300s.

Halley, 1910, based on photo.

Computer-generated image of Halley, 1986.

29

More Books About Comets and Meteors

Here are more books about comets and meteors. If you are interested in them, check your library or bookstore.

Asimov's Guide to Halley's Comet. Asimov (Walker)
The Asteroids. Asimov (Gareth Stevens)
Comet. Sagan (Random House)
Comets. Hamer (Watts)
Comets and Meteors. Couper (Franklin Watts)
Comets, Asteroids, and Meteors. Fradin (Childrens Press)
Did Comets Kill the Dinosaurs? Asimov (Gareth Stevens)
Fire and Ice: A History of Comets in Art. Olsen (Walker)
How Did We Find Out About Comets? Asimov (Avon)

Places to Visit

You can explore the Universe — including the places where comets, meteoroids, and asteroids roam — without leaving Earth. Here are some museums and centers where you can find many different kinds of space exhibits.

Bernice P. Bishop Museum and Planetarium
Honolulu, Hawaii

University of Arkansas-Little Rock
    Planetarium
Little Rock, Arkansas

London Children's Science Museum
London, Ontario

Koch Science Center and Planetarium
Evansville, Indiana

The Science Center of Iowa
Des Moines, Iowa

Astrocentre
Royal Ontario Museum
Toronto, Canada

For More Information About Comets and Meteors

Here are some people you can write to for more information about comets and meteors. Be sure to tell them exactly what you want to know about. And include your full name and address so they can write back to you.

For information about comets, meteoroids, and asteroids:
National Space Society
600 Maryland Avenue SW
Washington, DC 20024

Star Date
McDonald Observatory
Austin, Texas 78712

About missions to the comets and the asteroids:
NASA Kennedy Space Center
Educational Services Office
Kennedy Space Center, Florida 32899

NASA Jet Propulsion Laboratory
Public Affairs 180-201
4800 Oak Grove Drive
Pasadena, California 91109

For catalogs of slides, posters, and other astronomy material:
AstroMedia Order Department
21027 Crossroads Circle
Waukesha, Wisconsin 53187

Sky Publishing Corporation
49 Bay State Road
Cambridge, Massachusetts 02238-1290

Glossary

asteroid: "star-like." The asteroids are very small planets made of rock or metal. There are thousands of them in our Solar system, and they mainly orbit the Sun in large numbers between Mars and Jupiter. But some show up elsewhere in the Solar system — some as meteoroids and some possibly as "captured" moons of planets such as Mars.

astronomer: a person involved in the scientific study of the Universe and its various bodies.

atmosphere: the gases that surround a planet, star, or moon.

billion: in North America — and in this book — the number represented by 1 followed by nine zeroes— 1,000,000,000. In some places, such as the United Kingdom (Britain), this number is called "a thousand million." In these places, one billion would then be represented by 1 followed by *12* zeroes— 1,000,000,000,000: a million million, a number known as a trillion in North America.

comet: an object made of ice, rock, and gas; has a vapor tail that may be seen when the comet's orbit brings it close to the Sun.

crater: a hole or pit on a planet or moon created by volcanic explosions or the impact of meteorites.

evaporate: the process that turns water into a vapor or gas.

fireballs: meteors whose entry into Earth's atmosphere is bright and spectacular.

gravity: the force that causes objects like the Earth and Moon to be attracted to one another.

Halley's Comet: comet which passes by Earth on an average of every 76.1 years. Named for Edmund Halley, the English astronomer (1656-1742), it is especially notable in that every pass by this comet has been documented since its first definite recorded sighting by the Chinese in 240 BC. Its last pass by Earth occurred in 1986.

meteor: a meteoroid that has entered Earth's atmosphere. Also, the bright streak of light made as the meteoroid enters or moves through the atmosphere.

meteor shower: a concentrated group of meteors, seen when the Earth's orbit intersects debris from a comet.

meteorite: a meteoroid when it hits Earth.

meteoroid: a lump of rock or metal drifting through space. Meteoroids can be as big as asteroids or as small as specks of dust.

Newton, Sir Isaac: English natural philosopher (1642-1727) who discovered the Law of Gravity.

orbit: the path that one celestial object follows as it circles, or revolves, around another.

prehistoric: from the time in history before writing was invented.

probe: a craft that travels in space, photographing celestial bodies and even landing on some of them.

shooting star: a visual meteor appearing as a temporary streak of light in the night sky.

star: a mass of material, usually wholly gaseous, massive enough to initiate (or to have once initiated) nuclear reactions in its central regions.

Sun: our star and provider of the energy that makes life possible on Earth.

vapor: a gas formed from a solid or liquid. On Earth, clouds are made from water vapor.

Index

The publishers wish to thank the following for permission to reproduce copyright material: front cover, © Paul Dimare; p. 4, © Denis Milon; pp. 5, 8, © Keith Ward, 1989; p. 6 (large), © Mark Paternostro; p. 6 (inset), © Garret Moore, 1987; pp. 7, 29 (bottom), courtesy of NASA; p. 9 (top), © Helen and Richard Lines; p. 9 (inset), © Michael Carroll; p. 10 (large), © Mark Maxwell, 1989; p. 10 (inset), © Julian Baum, 1988; p. 11, courtesy of AIP Niels Bohr Library; pp. 12-13, photograph by Matthew Groshek, © Gareth Stevens, Inc., 1989; p. 12 (top), 13 (right), © Edward J. Olsen; pp. 14-15 (large), 16 (large), 20-21 (large), Mary Evans Picture Library; p. 14 (inset), Historical Pictures Service, Chicago; p. 16 (inset), © Alan McClure; p. 17, Yerkes Observatory Photographs; pp. 18-19 (background), 20 (lower), © Gareth Stevens, Inc., 1989; pp. 18 (inset), 19 (upper), courtesy of Jet Propulsion Laboratory, International Halley Watch; p. 19 (lower) © Max Planck Institute, Germany; p. 20 (upper), Neg. # 282680, courtesy Department of Library Services, American Museum of Natural History; p. 22 (all), Naval Research Laboratory; p. 23 (large), © Paul Dimare, 1987; pp. 23 (inset), 27 (all), 28 (all), 29 (top and center), © Anne Norcia, 1985; p. 24 (large), © Bruce Bond; p. 24 (inset), US Geological Survey, courtesy of Don E. Wilhelms and Donald E. Davis; p. 25, © Joe Tucciarone, 1987; p. 26 (large), © Max Planck Institute, Germany, courtesy of Ball Aerospace; p. 26 (inset), National Radio Astronomy Observatories/AUI; p. 27, Jet Propulsion Laboratory.

ISAAC ASIMOV'S
LIBRARY OF THE UNIVERSE

Cover Photo: © *THE IMAGE BANK*/ Geoff Gove

A panoramic introduction to space, this series offers fascinating current information and stunning full-color artwork and photography. It is the perfect resource for school reports.

Special features include:

- An index and a glossary of key terms and concepts
- A "Fact File"—space and science fact reference section
- Special "Amazing Facts" and "Unexplained Mysteries" sections
- Exciting and informative discussions of space facts and theories

COMETS AND METEORS

Why aren't the comets of today as spectacular as the ones from a generation ago? How are "shooting stars" related to comets? In this book, Isaac Asimov looks at those things that have long been streaking across our skies, filling us with wonder and sometimes. comets and meteors, celestial visitors bring about the cosmos—and about the origins of own Earth.

Isaac Asimov is the popular author of more science and science-fiction books for childre

A YEARLING NONFICTION BOOK•DELL PUBLISHING•NEW YORK

RL: 3.3
007-010
0-440-40450-9

ISBN 0-440-40450-9